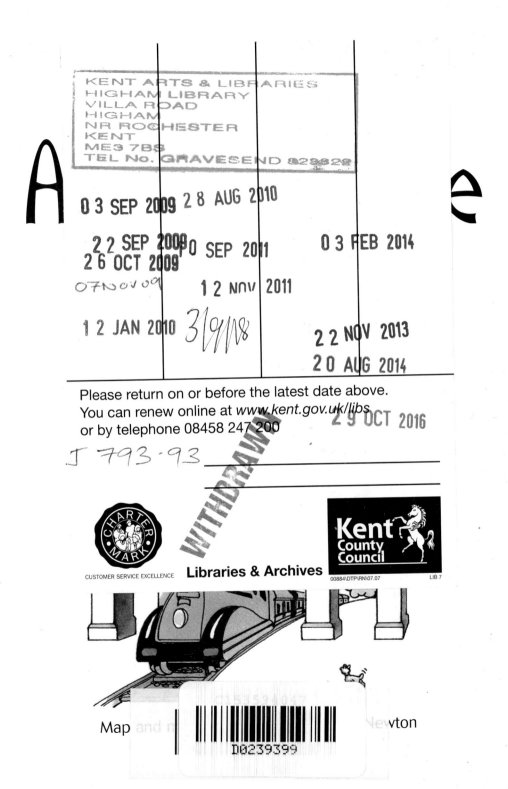

Please return on or before the latest date above.
You can renew online at *www.kent.gov.uk/libs*
or by telephone 08458 247 200

Map and ... Newton

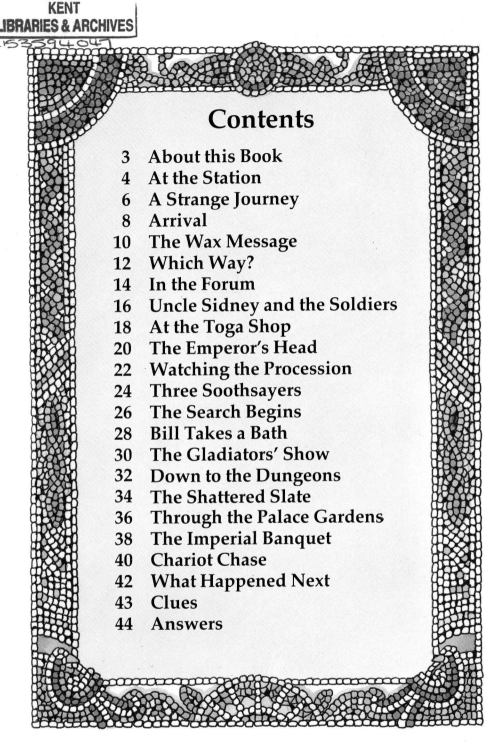

Contents

3   About this Book
4   At the Station
6   A Strange Journey
8   Arrival
10   The Wax Message
12   Which Way?
14   In the Forum
16   Uncle Sidney and the Soldiers
18   At the Toga Shop
20   The Emperor's Head
22   Watching the Procession
24   Three Soothsayers
26   The Search Begins
28   Bill Takes a Bath
30   The Gladiators' Show
32   Down to the Dungeons
34   The Shattered Slate
36   Through the Palace Gardens
38   The Imperial Banquet
40   Chariot Chase
42   What Happened Next
43   Clues
44   Answers

About this Book

Time Train to Ancient Rome is an exciting adventure story with a difference. The difference is that you can take part in the adventure.

Throughout the book, there are lots of tricky puzzles and perplexing problems for you to solve. You will need to find the answers to understand the next episode in the story.

Look at the pictures carefully and watch out for vital clues. Sometimes you will need to flick back through the book to help you find an answer.

There are extra clues on page 43 and you can check your answers on pages 44 to 48.

Just turn the page to begin the adventure.

At the Station

Lucy and Bill ran through the station towards the train on platform number 13. They dashed past the ticket barrier and sprinted down the last flight of steps just as the guard raised his flag. It was then that Lucy noticed several odd things and some even odder people on the platform. She wanted to stop and take a closer look, but there was no time to lose.

How many odd things and people can you spot?

5

A Strange Journey

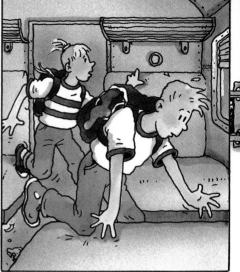

They leapt aboard and the guard blew his whistle. The train lurched forwards and steamed out of the station.

Bill and Lucy were off to stay with their Uncle Sidney in Grimbledon. Lucy wasn't looking forward to it very much. She gazed out of the window as the train left the town behind and tried not to think about the long, boring days ahead.

All of a sudden, the train plunged into a tunnel and everything went black. The tunnel wasn't very long, but when they reached the other end, the view through the window was somehow different. The trees and the fields were normal enough, but the things and the people looked strangely old-fashioned. And as the train gathered speed, they seemed to grow stranger and older.

They travelled on and on through the unknown landscape until, many hours later, they rounded a sweeping bend and the train began to slow down. Magnificent white stone buildings lined the track as the train wheezed to a halt. Bill and Lucy grabbed their rucksacks and made for the door.

7

Arrival

They stepped off the train on to a gleaming, white platform. They knew at once that something was very wrong. Grimbledon Station had never looked like this before.

It was all very odd. Bill and Lucy could hardly believe what they were seeing and hearing. All around them, people were chattering in a strange-sounding language and their clothes were extraordinary.

DISCESSUS
I ATHENAS
II MYCENAE
V BABYLONEM

ROMA

ROMA

STOLAE

Salve, Domine.

Cooee Metella

PRONUNTIATIONES

Videte urbem curru; hic tesserae.

8

The Wax Message

Uncle Sidney was nowhere to be seen. They waited ... and waited ... and waited. Then they walked out to the main entrance and looked up and down the street. But there was still no sign of him.

All of a sudden, a boy in a loin cloth sprinted up to them, holding out a brown, leather sack. He thrust it into Bill's hands, said something very fast in a funny foreign language and sped off again.

Lucy untied the sack and emptied the contents onto the ground. There was a scroll of thick paper, a handful of coins, two small, golden charms and a wooden-framed wax slate. Row after row of capital letters were carved into the wax. At first they made no sense at all, but bit by bit, Bill deciphered the strange message.

Can you work out the message on the wax slate?

Here you can see the contents
of the leather sack.

```
W E Y T S N G E X E I O S N C M S U A
E M O I O I B N P M N P S U L R S G G
L O U O R T U U E T T S I M E A H N E
C R L T R I T P C E H A B O S H O A P
O T L D Y A I U T E E N L R P C U L R
M N S E T W V D E M F O E F S N L E O
E E O S O U E L D E O O W E T E D H B
T I O U K O B E L S R S I V H D S T L
O C N T E Y E H Y A U S T O E L O E E
A N G E E P E N P E L M A H L G O L V M
```

Which Way?

Bill was puzzled. Should he believe the wax message or was it some sort of joke? Lucy picked up one of the golden charms and slipped the chain around her neck. All at once, as if by magic, the mysterious foreign chatter turned into words she could speak and understand.

"Now let's find Uncle Sidney," she said in the strange new language, as Bill fastened the other charm around his neck.

They left the station and set off down a cobbled road. They were in the country, but in the distance they saw the walls and buildings of a city. Lucy stopped for a moment and looked around. She delved into the sack, and pulled out the scroll. It was a map.

"We're here," she said, pointing. "We know where we're going, so we just need to find the shortest route."

Which is the shortest route?

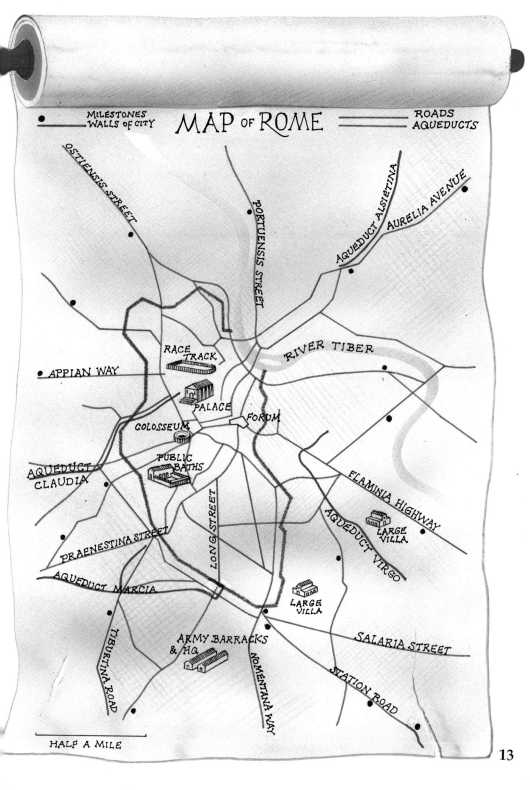

In the Forum

The scroll map led them into a large, open square surrounded by grand-looking buildings. It was packed with people rushing about making a lot of noise.

"This must be the forum," said Lucy. "But where's Uncle Sidney?"

Can you spot Uncle Sidney?

15

Uncle Sidney and the Soldiers

Lucy spotted Uncle Sidney first. She grabbed Bill's arm and together they dashed across the bustling forum. Uncle Sidney was standing in the middle of a group of mean-looking soldiers, wearing what appeared to be a baggy yellow sheet. He looked very cross and was shouting at the soldiers at the top of his voice.

> What? Arrest me? Certainly not. I am Sidonius and the Emperor's my friend.

> Who are these barbarian brats? Push off or we'll arrest you too.

> Billius and Lucilla – my nephew and niece. They've just arrived on the Time Train.

Uncle Sidney peered out over a mass of helmets and caught sight of Bill and Lucy. He broke away from the soldiers and stepped forwards, smiling. The soldiers glared and took a step forwards, too. Bill and Lucy stood rooted to the spot, not knowing what to say and unable to believe their ears.

Suddenly, Uncle Sidney grabbed their hands and began to run. He zigzagged back across the forum, leaving the astonished soldiers behind, shouting and waving their spears. Bill and Lucy bombarded their Uncle with questions. But Uncle Sidney said nothing. He smiled mysteriously and kept on running.

> Sidonius? Billius? I don't understand.

> Time train? Barbarians? What's going on?

At last they stopped to catch their breath and Uncle Sidney began to talk. Lucy hoped he might explain why they had arrived in Ancient Rome instead of Grimbledon, but he didn't. Instead, he told them a strange story about the Emperor, Fabulus Caesar, and the terrible things that were happening in Rome . . .

Sorry about the detour but things are bad here in Rome. The Emperor's soldiers are arresting all his old friends and no one is safe.

OUCH! My toe.

"I is 1, V is 5 and X is 10," he explained. "II is 2, III is 3, XX is 20 and so on. When you see a smaller number in front of a bigger number you subtract it from the bigger one, so IV is 4. When you see a smaller number after a bigger number you add them together, which means VI is 6."

All of a sudden, a large pebble hurtled towards them, landing with a thump on Uncle Sidney's foot. Bill picked it up and noticed a series of letters and dots scrawled on its surface. Perhaps it was some sort of message. Uncle Sidney agreed and explained that the letters I, V and X were Roman numbers.

XVI· XII· V· I· XIX· V· VIII·
V· XII· XVI· XIII· V· IX· I· XII·
II· V· IX· XIV· VII· VIII· V· XII·
IV· I· XIX· I· XVI· XVIII· IX· XIX·
XV· XIV· V· XVIII· XIII· XXV·
XIV· XXI· XIII· II· V· XVIII· IX·
XIX· XIV· IX· XIV· V· XX·
XXV· X IV· IX· XIV·V·
VI· XVIII· XV· XIII·
VI· III·

Can you decipher the message on the pebble?

17

At the Toga Shop

Bill and Lucy soon decoded the strange message.

"But who's it from?" asked Bill. "And what should we do about it?"

"We must make a plan," said Uncle Sidney, slipping the pebble into his cloak. "But first of all you must get rid of your Barbarian clothes."

Uncle Sidney led them into a small shop jam-packed with bales of cloth, off-the-peg tunics and cut-price cloaks. The shopkeeper stared in amazement at Bill and Lucy's strange clothes while Uncle Sidney explained what they needed.

"A tunic and a toga for Billius," he said. "A stola and a palla for Lucilla, and two pairs of sandals."

The shopkeeper and his assistants set to work, with tape measures, pins and needles. Meanwhile, Uncle Sidney crept out of the shop and set off to discuss the strange pebble message with his friend the sculptor.

18

In no time at all, Bill and Lucy were kitted out in real Roman clothes. Bill was very pleased with his new outfit, but Lucy wasn't so sure. Her dress was made of funny itchy material and the cloak kept slipping off.

Next the shopkeeper led them into the shoe department at the back of the shop. Bill chose a pair of yellow sports sandals and strutted around the shop admiring his new Roman feet.

Bill pulled out some shining coins from the leather sack and turned round to find the shopkeeper emptying baskets of assorted sandals all over the floor. Lucy was sitting on a bench with one red sandal on her right foot.

"I know I've seen the other one somewhere," said the shopkeeper.

Can you find Lucy's missing sandal?

The Emperor's Head

They found Uncle Sidney in a sculptor's studio just up the road. He was standing in a famous-person position on a low table, keeping very still.

The sculptor's name was Bustamarbellus, or Busta for short. He was hammering away at a great big block of stone which was starting to take the shape of Uncle Sidney's head.

Bill and Lucy gazed at the peculiar collection of stone carvings that crammed the studio. There were horses' heads and human heads, bits of legs and broken toes.

"Who are all these people?" asked Lucy, gazing at a row of stone heads.

"Important Romans," said Uncle Sidney, almost without opening his mouth. "Just like me."

"The Emperor's head is here too," said the sculptor. "It's a perfect likeness. He's the one with the bushy eyebrows and not much hair."

Where is the Emperor's head?

Watching the Procession

All of a sudden, the sound of trumpets and people cheering filled the street outside. A procession was passing by. They all dashed upstairs to get a better view.

"It's the Emperor," cried Uncle Sidney, wishing he wasn't so short-sighted.

Bill and Lucy stared at the man in the purple toga. Something was wrong...

"Oh no," gasped Busta. "This can only mean one thing."

What's wrong?

BVSTAMARBELLVS
SCVLPTOR

THE SCROLL SHOP

23

Three Soothsayers

One hour later, Uncle Sidney, Bill and Lucy arrived at a cave in a rocky hillside just outside the city. This was the home of the famous three soothsayers. If anybody could help solve the mystery of the Emperor's imposter, they could.

"Ten denarii per consultation," growled the grumpy guard at the entrance.

Bill handed over ten silver coins and the guard led them into a gloomy cave where they found three funny old men sitting on stone blocks.

"A friend of mine has been replaced by an imposter," Uncle Sidney explained. "Do you know what has happened to him?"

Your friend has been kidnapped by a rogue apple seller. Follow the milestones past the fighting gladiators to the steaming thermal springs. Beware the Ides of March.

PHIBBER

The soothsayers gave their answers at once, but to Bill and Lucy's surprise, each one was different.

"Only one of them is telling the truth," growled the guard. "The other two are lying."

"Do they always do this?" asked Lucy, amazed.

"Always," said the guard. "But a different one tells the truth each time."

Lucy gave the guard another ten coins and spoke to the soothsayers.

"Which one of you told Uncle Sidney the truth?" she asked.

Which of the soothsayers is telling the truth this time? Which one told Uncle Sidney the truth?

Your friend is safe. You will find him in the baths, disguised as an apple seller and protected by gladiators bearing the sign of the serpent. Beware of the shattered slate.

FRAUDUM

SPUR   SPURIUS

Your friend is a prisoner and must fight for his life. An apple seller's gift and a numbered stone will lead you to him. Listen carefully to the voices in the steam or disaster will follow. Beware the sign of the serpent

Not me. I didn't.

Phibber is lying.

Fraudum did.

The Search Begins

They scrambled down the rocky hillside wondering what the soothsayer's cryptic message meant and where to start their search.

"What's a numbered stone?" asked Bill feeling very confused.

"Perhaps it's a milestone," said Uncle Sidney. "Then there's steam in the baths and apple sellers in the er ..."

"Market?" Lucy suggested.

They decided to split up. Bill ran to the baths, Uncle Sidney set off on a milestone search and Lucy headed for the market.

Fifteen minutes and thirty apples later, she was standing in a queue. The lady in front was buying enough fruit and vegetables to feed the Roman army and the boy behind the stall was trying hard to work out how much it all cost.

"Hurry up," said the lady, grabbing the boy's wax slate.

Lucy glanced at the slate over the lady's shoulder. She felt sorry for the boy. Roman numbers were hard to add up quickly and Roman money was tricky too – four asses made one sestertius and four, sestertii made one denarius.

"It's obvious," said the lady. "It comes to six denarii."

"No it doesn't," cried Lucy.

Is Lucy correct? How much should the lady pay?

PLUMS : VIII S.
LETTUCE : XII A
CABBAGE : XIV A
LEMONS : III S
APPLES : IX A
GRAPES : XV A
EXOTIC FRUIT : II D

TOTAL

Bill Takes a Bath

Roman baths weren't like ordinary baths. Bill hadn't a clue what to do or where to go, so he decided to follow everyone else. He took off his clothes and wrapped himself in a towel. Then he walked through an open area where men were wrestling into a hot room filled with steam.

All of a sudden, he overheard two men talking in low, secretive voices. He thought nothing of it at first, but as he walked into an even hotter, steamier room, his heart sank.

Through the steam he caught the unmistakable sight of a serpent tattooed on to a

man's arm. The arm belonged to one of the men he had overheard moments before.

The two men left the steam and Bill followed, listening to all they said. First they went into a room where slaves scraped the dirt off their backs, then they swam in a warm indoor pool followed by a dip in an outdoor pool filled with freezing cold water. By now Bill had heard enough. He had to hurry back and warn the others.

This special picture shows Bill and the two men in each room in the baths. Can you follow their suspicious conversation?

The Gladiators' Show

Meanwhile, back at the market, the fruit boy was beaming. He thanked Lucy over and over again and handed her a juicy red apple and a small disc made of clay.

This was it! The apple seller's gift. But what was it? The boy explained that the disc was a ticket to the gladiators' show at the Colosseum. He pointed to a large, circular building in the distance. Lucy thanked him and sped off to join the crowds heading for the Colosseum.

Lucy handed her ticket to the man at the turnstile, keeping her ears and eyes open for some sort of clue that would lead her to the Emperor. The show was just about to begin and the first prisoner was led up from the dungeons to fight Daddio Maximus, the gladiator champion.

Several minutes later

The prisoner lunged at his opponent and the crowd began to roar. At the same time, Lucy remembered the soothsayer's words. Suddenly they all made sense and Lucy knew that the Emperor was one of the prisoners waiting to fight the dreaded Daddio Maximus. There was no time to lose.

PRISONERS' NUMBERS	CELL NUMBERS
XIV	XXI
XXVIII	XVIII
XXXI	VI
XLIX	XI
LVI	XIV
LXV	XXV
LXXVII	XXXIV
LXXXIV	IX
XCIX	XL

As she crept towards the dungeons, Lucy spotted a list of numbers on a notice board. One of them was very familiar. In a flash of inspiration, she realized that the pebble message was the "numbered stone" and that it had come from the Emperor.

Which number is familiar?

Down to the Dungeons

Lucy slipped through the entrance into a gloomy passage that sloped steeply downwards. The air was damp and chilly and the further she went, the darker it became. At the bottom of the slope, she came to a junction with passages running right, left and straight ahead.

The only light came from a flickering candle. Beside it was a slab of intricately carved marble set into the wall. Lucy picked up the candle to take a closer look.

All of a sudden, she realized that the circular pattern in the centre of the slab was a plan of the dungeons showing a maze of passages and lots of little cells.

Only five of the cells were numbered, but she was sure that the numbers followed a pattern. If only she could work out the numbering system, she could locate the Emperor's cell and trace a route to it

What route should Lucy take to get to the Emperor's cell?

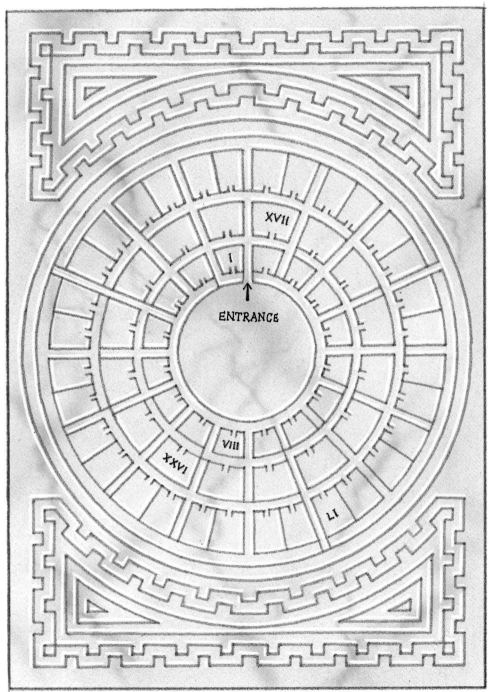

33

The Shattered Slate

Lucy tugged at the rusty bolt and heaved the heavy cell door open to find the Emperor inside, dressed in a gladiator's outfit. He was very surprised to see Lucy. She explained who she was and together they retraced Lucy's route through the dungeons to the entrance into the arena.

Lucy threw her cloak over the Emperor's head as a disguise. Then they slipped silently past the guard into the crowds of cheering spectators. They made a dash for the exit and sprinted through the streets of Rome until they arrived, panting and gasping, at the sculptor's studio.

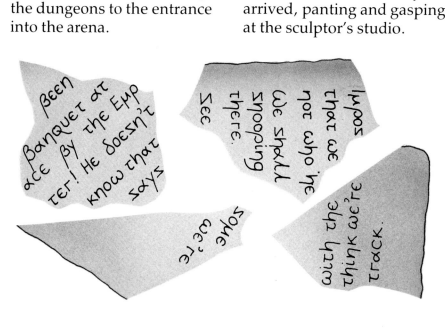

Here they found Bill looking very worried. Uncle Sidney and the sculptor were nowhere to be seen. They had left a message on a clay slate, but Bill couldn't decipher the sculptor's handwriting.

He held up the slate to show them. But suddenly... SMASH!

He dropped it. It fell to the ground and shattered into little pieces.

"It's alright," said Lucy, kneeling down. "We can match all the pieces together."

What does the sculptor's message say?

PS
while
on the
summoned
the
errors

wrong
stone. I
No luck
you later
so
while

We have know
to a pad
he's
he is.

Through the Palace Gardens

Uncle Sidney and the sculptor were in grave danger. There was no time to lose. They had to get to the palace and stop the banquet. But how?

"I know a way into the palace," said the Emperor, smiling. "Quick. Follow me."

He led them through the back streets of Rome to the walls of the palace gardens. Bill and Lucy peered over the wall and the Emperor explained that the door on the far right was always left unlocked.

Now all they needed to do was find a way through the gardens out of sight of the guards.

Can you find a safe route?

The Imperial Banquet

Inside the palace, the Emperor led them through a series of magnificent corridors towards the imperial dining room. Bill and Lucy burst into the room, just as the banquet was about to begin.

"STOP!" yelled Bill. "The food is poisoned and the Emperor's a fake."

The two men from the baths glared at Bill, but the fake Emperor just laughed and carried on munching.

Uncle Sidney and the sculptor knew that Bill was telling the truth, but the other guests weren't sure.

Bill did some quick thinking. The only way to convince them was to prove the food was poisoned. And the only way to do that was to offer a plate of poisoned food to the fake Emperor. Bill knew he would refuse. But which dish was poisoned?

Bill thought back to the baths and recalled a strange word. In his mind, he began to rearrange the letters . . .

Which food is poisoned?

Chariot Chase

The fake Emperor's grin became a grimace, and just as Bill expected, he refused the plate of poisoned food. At once, the other guests knew that Bill was telling the truth.

The fake Emperor roared with anger, tossed the plate into the air and kicked over a whole table of food. Bill went flying along with the food and landed with a bump. He sat up, seeing stars, to find Uncle Sidney, the sculptor and the Emperor tying up the fake Emperor's evil accomplices.

Then Lucy spotted the fake Emperor making a quick getaway. She yelled to Bill and the two of them chased after him. Too late. He jumped into an empty chariot and raced away. But Lucy and Bill weren't beaten yet. They sped down the steps to the street and did exactly the same.

"Quick," said Lucy to the driver. "Follow that chariot."

Bill and Lucy clung on tightly as the chariot sped after the fake Emperor out of the city and on to the road that led to the station.

The chariot pulled up on the forecourt. Bill and Lucy leapt out and rushed into the station which was packed with people.

"There he is," cried Bill. "We've got to catch him before it's too late."

Where is he?

What Happened Next

Lucy and Bill jumped aboard in hot pursuit. But all of a sudden, the door slammed shut behind them with a bang and the train lurched forwards with a sudden jolt…

The next thing they knew, the train was slowing down at a station. Bill opened his eyes, feeling very bleary and confused. The train stopped and everyone got out.

Bill and Lucy walked across the platform in a daze –

straight into the arms of Uncle Sidney! He greeted them with a wink and led them away without a word. Lucy didn't know what to think. Was it all a dream? She looked down at her feet – perhaps not. But if it wasn't a dream…

She turned round to look at the train for the last time and smiled as she caught sight of the fake Emperor in the midst of the crowded platform..

Can you see the fake Emperor?

Clues

Pages 4-5
This is easy. Use your eyes.

Pages 8-9
Uncle Sidney is describing the station from the opposite direction. A sundial is used to tell the time.

Pages 10-11
Read the first column of letters downwards and the second column upwards, and so on.

Pages 12-13
The milestone pinpoints their position. Use a ruler or a piece of thread to find the shortest route.

Pages 14-15
Remember Uncle Sidney wears glasses.

Pages 16-17
Try replacing the numbers with letters. Here are the Roman numbers 1 to 26.

I	II	III	IV	V	VI
VII	VIII	IX	X	XI	XII
XIII	XIV	XV	XVI	XVII	XVIII
XIX	XX	XXI	XXII	XXIII	XXIV
XXV	XXVI				

Pages 18-19
Look for a sandal of the same size, shape and colour as the one on Lucy's right foot.

Pages 20-21
This is easy. Use your eyes.

Pages 22-23
Compare the Emperor's face with the stone head on pages 20-21.

Pages 24-25
This is very tricky. Look at the answers to Lucy's question. Then test each soothsayer's answer in turn to see if he could be telling the truth while the other two are lying.

Pages 26-27
A = asses, D = denarii, S = sestertii.

Pages 28-29
Look for the sign of the serpent.

Pages 30-31
Look at the pebble message on pages 16-17. L is 50 and C is 100 in Roman numerals.

Pages 32-33
The inner circle of cells are numbered anticlockwise.

Pages 34-35
Trace the shattered bits or photocopy the page and cut them out. Then piece them together.

Pages 36-37
They can crawl behind hedges and use plants as cover to keep out of the guards' sight.

Pages 38-39
Look for the strange word in the suspicious conversation on pages 28-29. Rearrange the letters to find out which food is poisoned.

Pages 40-41
This is easy. Look for the soles of his shoes.

Page 42
Look for the Emperor's face.

Answers

Pages 4-5

The strange things and people are ringed in black.

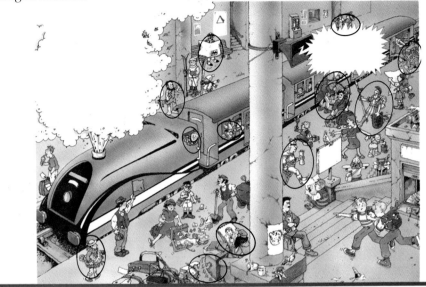

Pages 8-9

Bill and Lucy should meet Uncle Sidney beneath the sundial. This is a sort of clock which uses a shadow cast by the sun to show the time. Uncle Sidney's right and left are reversed because he is describing the station from the opposite direction.

Pages 10-11

The letters in the wax message read downwards in the first column, upwards in the second column and so on. This is what it says:

WELCOME TO ANCIENT ROME. YOU'LL SOON GET USED TO IT. SORRY TO KEEP YOU WAITING BUT I'VE BEEN HELD UP UNEXPECTEDLY. PLEASE MEET ME IN THE FORUM AS SOON AS POSSIBLE.

WITH LOVE FROM UNCLE S.

PS THE GOLDEN CHARMS SHOULD SOLVE THE LANGUAGE PROBLEM.

Pages 12-13

The shortest route to the forum is marked in black.

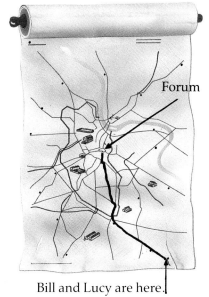

Forum

Bill and Lucy are here.

Pages 14-15

Here is Uncle Sidney.

Pages 16-17

Each number stands for a letter. I(1)=A, II(2)=B and so on. Here is the message with spaces and punctuation marks added.

Please help me. I am being held as a prisoner. My number is ninety nine. From F.C.

Pages 18-19

The missing sandal is ringed in black.

Pages 20-21

The Emperor's head is ringed in black.

Pages 22-23

The Emperor's face, particularly his nose, is not the same as the stone head on pages 20-21. This must mean that the man wearing the Emperor's clothes is not the Emperor, but an imposter.

The Emperor's stone head

The imposter

Pages 24-25

Fraudum is telling Lucy the truth. This means that Phibber is lying to Lucy which in turn means that Fraudum lied to Uncle Sidney. Spurius is also lying to Lucy which means that the opposite of what he says to her is the truth. In other words, Spurius DID answer Uncle Sidney's question truthfully.

(If you got this one right, you're a genius.)

Pages 26-27

The total comes to 50 asses, 11 sestertii and 2 denarii. This is equal to 7 denarii, 3 sestertii and 2 asses. The lady is trying to get away with paying less than she owes.

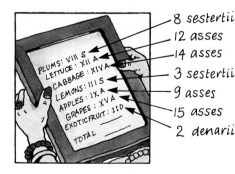

PLUMS: VIII S — 8 sestertii
LETTUCE: XII A — 12 asses
CABBAGE: XIV A — 14 asses
LEMONS: III S — 3 sestertii
APPLES: IX A — 9 asses
GRAPES: XV A — 15 asses
EXOTIC FRUIT: II D — 2 denarii

TOTAL

Pages 28-29

You can spot the two men holding the suspicious conversation by the serpent signs tattooed on their arms. Here is their suspicious conversation:

"The banquet is arranged.
All the guests will die."
"When?"
"Today."
"At the palace?"
"Correct."
"Where's the poison?"
"It's only in the HUMMOROSS.
Get it?"
"I see."

Pages 30-31

The number 99 is familiar. In his pebble message on pages 16-17, the Emperor says that he is a prisoner with the number 99. The notice board shows that prisoner number 99 is in cell number 40.

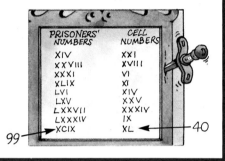

Pages 32-33

Lucy's route is shown in black.

Pages 34-35

When the shattered slate is pieced together, the message reads as follows:

We have been summoned to a banquet at the palace by the Emperor's imposter! He doesn't know that we know that he's not who he says he is. We shall do some snooping while we're there. See you later.

PS No luck with the milestone. I think we're on the wrong track.

Pages 36-37

The safe route through the gardens is marked in black.

Pages 38-39

The crooks in the baths said that only the HUMMOROSS were poisoned. If you rearrange the letters, this word becomes MUSHROOMS.

Pages 40-41

Here is the fake Emperor.

Page 42

Like Bill and Lucy, the fake Emperor is now in modern clothes.